1001 QUESTIONS

Valerie Christie

Helper Petrie Publishing

ISBN: 0615846327
ISBN-13: 978-0615846323

DEDICATION

This is for Myrtle.
I miss you.

ACKNOWLEDGMENTS

Thank you to Aezariel for reading and actually answering each of the questions from which this book is derived. You're the one who should be writing books.

Thank you to Edward Holden for helping with the layout.

INTRODUCTION

I have lots of questions but very few answers.

How you choose to use this text and interpret its content is up to you. A lot of the questions can be understood in different ways and invite follow ups such as "when?" or "why?" Whether you decide to probe – and how deeply - is your decision. Similarly you will have to agree whether or not to accept "neither" or "both" as possible answers for either/or style questions. I have designed the book so text only appears on one side of each page. This is intended to allow readers to cut out individual questions for use in games. Again whether you keep the book intact or cut it up is for you to decide.

1001 QUESTIONS

Chunky or creamy peanut butter?

Do you use or believe in any forms of alternative medicine?

Do you have anything hanging from your rear-view mirror?

What is the biggest advantage you have going for you?

Quality or quantity?

Does every question have an answer?

Do you have any phobias?

Would you rather go camping or stay in a hotel?

How old were you when you learned to ride a bicycle?

Do you think it is worse to kill a policeman than it is to kill any other human being?

What would you do if you accidentally saw the answer to a difficult test problem on a classmate's exam?

Have you ever posted graffiti?

Have you ever inherited anything from anyone?

Name a place you visited that did not live up to your expectations.

Have you ever had to call a locksmith?

If you were in a successful band what would you ask to have in your dressing room?

Would you rather deep sea dive or sky dive?

What is the best stress reliever you know?

Is there someone you would like to apologize to?

Have you ever done something on a dare?

What are your thoughts about the saying "better late than never?"

Have you ever been to a rodeo?

Have you ever been in a car accident?

What do you think of the paparazzi?

Do you like clowns?

Why do you think chewing gum comes in sweet and minty flavors, but not savory?

Do you pick up hitchhikers?

Is orange soda named after the color or the fruit?

Hamburgers or cheeseburgers?

Have you ever stayed in a bed and breakfast?

Do you follow your heart or your head?

How do you know right from wrong?

What is your favorite soft drink?

What characteristics or personality traits are most important to you in a politician?

What do you think would be on the world's best pizza?

Is it harder for you to forgive yourself or others?

If you were making a time capsule to be opened in 100 years, what 3 things would you put in it?

Have you ever had a black eye?

Name something you have always wanted that you will never ever have.

Have you ever belonged to a gym or fitness center?

If you believed one of your elderly parents was no longer able to drive safely, what would you do?

Have you ever read any science fiction novels?

Would you ever knowingly hire an undocumented immigrant?

What are your thoughts about country music?

Do you think people are basically good?

How many countries have you been to?

What is your favorite flavor of pie?

Is there any place that has been closed or torn down that you miss?

Who do you trust the most?

Is there a particular book or story that has had a big impact on your life?

What is the longest you have gone without speaking?

Do you like jelly beans? Are there any flavors you dislike?

Who was your first girlfriend or boyfriend?

Do you think electric cars will replace gas cars?

Do you like guacamole?

Should professional athletes be role models?

Have you read the entire Bible?

Do you know the name of your mailman?

If you were a pebble, what would you say to a boy throwing you into a pond?

Are you a sprinter or a marathoner?

What is the best meal you ever had?

Do your religious beliefs differ from those of your family members'?

Do you crack your knuckles?

Have you ever gone white water rafting?

If you were to get a tattoo what would it be?

Are you more of a motivator, entertainer, persuader, or teacher?

Do you think dreams have meaning?

If someone offered you $1,000 to kill a butterfly, would you do it?

Could you be content if you never have any children or nieces and nephews?

Did you ever have a tree house?

If you had a bumper sticker on your car, what would it say?

In general do men or women make better bosses?

Have you ever been to Manhattan?

Are you more intrigued by outer space or the oceans?

What do you think about cults?

Do you own a bicycle?

Who is the most interesting member of your family?

What is the fastest you have ever driven in a car?

Do you know how to unlock a door with a credit card?

Have you ever been bitten by fire ants?

What was the biggest opportunity you have ever passed up?

Would you rather watch TV alone or with other people?

Who do you think is really successful?

Have you ever captured fireflies?

Is justice or mercy more important?

Should the US fully convert to the metric system?

Name something that is so bad it is good.

What do you love most about your family?

What is the difference between garbage and trash?

If you were to become famous what do you (realistically) think would be the most likely reason?

Are your relatives mostly Democrats or Republicans?

What is your favorite Winter Olympic sport to watch?

Do you like cinnamon?

Are there any circumstances under which you would ever marry someone your parents disliked?

If you could choose any sound to be your alarm in the morning, what would you choose?

What living person do you admire the most?

Who is the friend you have had the longest?

If you bumped your car into another car, but nobody saw you do it, would you leave your name?

How do you keep up with current events?

Do you think a hate crime is worse than the same crime committed for non hate crime reasons?

If you had to associate spring with a symbol, what would it be?

Have you ever bought a product from an infomercial?

Have you ever gone to a hookah bar?

Have you ever met anyone famous?

Have you ever eaten octopus?

Have you ever worked as a waiter or waitress?

Have you ever considered joining the Peace Corps?

What is something you think you may be wrong about?

What is something that you want to try but think you might not be good at?

What do you think of televangelists?

Do you own any musical instruments?

What do you think about fishing as a sport?

Would you rather have $50,000 free and clear or $250,000 that is illegal?

Have you ever had a pet cat?

Would you rather have an attic or a basement?

Do you prefer women who are extremely pale or deeply tanned?

Can courage exist in the absence of fear?

If you had a boat, what would you name it?

If you could ask the devil one question, or tell him one thing, what would it be?

Do you typically doubt or trust your intuition?

What common job would you never do no matter how much it paid?

Do you like rollercoasters?

Who is you favorite actor?

What is the most beautiful thing you have ever seen?

Would you rather be an advertising executive or an IRS agent?

Have you ever sung karaoke?

If you could ask any one of your deceased ancestors a question, who would it be and what would you ask?

Green or red apples?

What is the best compliment you have ever received?

Are you concerned about developing a specific illness or disability?

How would you like to experience your 15 minutes of fame?

If you were cooking for someone very important to you, what would you make?

Do computers save time or do they just make us waste more time?

Do you like candy canes?

Is it ever right to tell a lie?

Do you believe in karma?

Who has more power, the government or the people?

Have you ever read anything by Tom Clancy?

Do you think kids raised by single parents are at a disadvantage?

How do you feel about talking on the phone?

Who do you think is the most overrated celebrity?

When people find out what you do for work, what question do they most often ask you?

If your parents lost all of their money would you let them move in with you?

How do you know right from wrong?

Do you like ice-cream with cake?

If you could have any personalized number plate, what would you get?

Would you rather be stranded on an island alone or with someone you dislike?

Do state lotteries exploit poor people?

Can you lick your elbow?

Do you like fried pickles?

What do you say to telemarketers when they call?

Do you believe that dreams can help us solve our problems?

Do you prefer going to a movie theater or waiting to be able to watch the movie at home?

When you lie why do you lie?

Do you typically pay a lot of attention to caloric and nutrition content when buying groceries?

If you had to wear a t-shirt with one word on it for the rest of your life, which word would you choose?

Have you ever been called for jury duty?

What is the funniest movie you have ever seen?

Do you usually iron and then hang up or fold your clean laundry?

Have you ever played Dungeons and Dragons?

Should the government restrict the size of sugary drinks that can be purchased?

What is something that you have only done once but are dying to do again?

If you were a tree, what would be carved into your trunk?

In your opinion, what is the most delicious fruit?

What makes you feel old?

Why do you think people of each generation like new music?

Who is the Prime Minister of the United Kingdom?

Have you ever eaten duck?

What type of information (if any) do you think a government should keep from its citizens?

If you had 20 seconds to talk someone out of killing themselves, what would you say?

When you were in grade school, what did you want to be when you grew up?

What is your least favorite household chore?

How do you vent your anger?

Have you ever been to Las Vegas?

Larry Bird or Michael Jordan?

In your opinion what has been the most important scientific discovery ever?

Are there really any selfless acts?

What three places would you take someone visiting your hometown?

If you could learn one skill without trying, what would it be?

When was the last time you fixed or repaired something?

How do you feel about buying products that were made in outside of the United States?

How much of success is just luck?

What do you think should be the eleventh Commandment?

Does speaking in front of crowds make you nervous?

When you pay for things do you set your money on the counter or hand it to the cashier?

If you owned a snake would you be able to feed it live animals?

If you were abandoned in the wilderness, would you survive?

Do you usually stop or try to make it through yellow lights?

Do you feel you have a purpose or calling in life?

What would you do if the couple next to you in a cinema kept talking during a movie?

If you were a rapper what would you call yourself?

Would you rather be highly educated or highly successful?

Have you ever eaten tofu?

All things being equal would you rather buy an American-made or foreign car?

What is the scariest movie you have ever seen?

Would you rather work really hard at an interesting job or take it easy at a dull job?

What is something you want to learn to do?

Do you prefer thick or thin crust pizza?

Can you remember sitting on a chair before your legs were long enough for your feet to touch the floor?

Do you like mayonnaise?

Is it better to buy or lease a new car?

Do you consider yourself to be a nerd?

How easily are you influenced by the moods and actions of others?

If you won a large lottery would you take a smaller lump sum or the total over 20 years?

Would you rather be in trouble with the CIA, the IRS, or the Mafia?

What is your favorite place in your home?

Have you ever driven a motorcycle?

If you were in a pageant, what would your talent be?

Did you ever get sent to the principal's office?

If you could ask God a question what would it be?

How often do you weigh yourself?

Would you change your religion for someone you loved?

Would you rather be on a plane with no parachutes or a sinking ship with no lifejackets or life boats?

Acoustic or electric guitars?

North Carolina basketball or Duke?

What do you like to dip chicken nuggets in?

What is your biggest weakness in life?

Scrambled, poached, or fried?

Should parents be held responsible when their kids commit crimes or fail to attend school?

What has been your greatest achievement in life so far?

What are your thoughts about celebrities who publicize their political views?

Do you think being a school teacher is a difficult job?

Should adults try to teach young people lessons or should they let them find out things on their own?

Would you sell your eggs or sperm?

Do you have any birthmarks?

How would you describe who God is to an alien who had never heard of him?

Why doesn't Tarzan have a beard?

If you were going to do karaoke tonight, what song would you sing?

What is something of absolutely no use that you intend to keep?

What is your favorite dessert?

Have you ever disliked someone and not known why?

Who would you like to see in concert?

Should elected officials vote based on their constituents' opinions or follow their consciences?

Who do you think is the greatest overall living athlete?

Can you think of a time when you have been frightened by the weather?

When does sound become music?

What is the best Italian restaurant in town?

Have you ever suspected that a friend or family member was really a secret agent?

If this were 1968 do you think you would be a hippie?

Were you named after anyone?

What is your favorite soup?

Is it true that money is the root of all evil?

Who do you go to for advice?

Do you typically answer your phone when it rings or let it go to voicemail then call back later?

Do you ever watch professional wrestling?

Are there any artificial sweeteners that you think really do taste as good as sugar?

How would you entertain yourself if stranded on a desert island?

Have you ever laughed so hard that you got tears in your eyes?

Strawberry or blueberry?

If you found a stray Pit Bull on your way home tomorrow what would you do?

Do you own a gun?

Almond Joy or Mounds?

Should online gambling be legal?

Do you know your license plate number by heart?

In what way do you hope you are like your father?

What is your opinion of mandatory, police enforced, curfews for young people?

What is something you know you do differently than most people?

What is truth?

Do you think a leader should be feared or liked?

What do you see yourself doing 5 years from now?

Do you ever pretend to not hear someone when you are really ignoring them?

Is happiness found or made?

Is attempted murder any less bad than murder?

How would you describe yourself during adolescence?

If money was not a consideration what career would you pursue?

Do you think smokers should be allowed to smoke indoors?

Rock, scissors, or paper?

What is the longest time you have gone without sleep?

What are your thoughts about George W. Bush?

Were you ever a boy or girl scout?

What is your favorite acronym?

Have you ever had to save someone by performing the Heimlich maneuver?

Have you ever gone to a professional football game?

If your life was a reality TV show, what would be the hook to would draw viewers in?

Cookies or brownies?

Have you ever smoked a cigar?

What religion were you raised in?

Is it good for parents to encourage children to believe in Santa Clause, the Easter Bunny, and the Tooth Fairy?

If it was somehow proven that we are living in a computer program, what do you think would happen?

What qualities are most important to you in elected officials?

Do you remember learning to read?

What would you do if your best friend married someone you disliked?

Do you believe in UFOs?

Should the American government financially support Olympic teams?

What is your favorite weird food combination?

As you get older, how has your definition of success changed?

What do you most admire about police officers?

What is the largest crowd you have ever been in?

Would you say that you are addicted to anything?

What is the most foolish thing you did in high school?

Does money equal freedom?

How often do you wash your car?

Do you have more male or female friends?

What responsibility do we have to conserve resources for future generations?

Have you ever seen a magic trick that seems impossible?

Are you ever hesitant to eat cake after someone has blown on it to put out the candles?

What was the most difficult test you have ever taken?

Would you prefer to live in the countryside or in a city?

Are you good at hiding your feelings?

Can a question ever really be answered with a question?

If you were wealthy would you hire an interior designer to decorate your house?

When was the last time you were deeply embarrassed?

How often do you strike up conversations with strangers?

Can you swim underwater with your eyes open?

Who will be liable if a self-driving car has an accident?

What is the worst job you have ever had?

What is your favorite winter sport to watch?

What song have you intentionally listened to the most number of times?

Do you ever break promises?

Do you often lose track of time?

What are some things your friends or family tease you about?

Have you ever done line dancing?

In what way are you most competitive?

What was the luckiest moment of your life?

If you were stranded on a desert island and could only bring 3 things what would they be?

Dine-in or to-go?

Do you have a lucky number?

Is there something they should just never be joked about...?

What life lesson did you learn the hard way?

Do you typically plan out your day or just take it as it comes?

If you could get paid to write a non-fiction book about anything, what would you write about?

If you were at the Pearly Gates, and God asked why he should let you in what would you say?

Would you rather be lost in a desert or a jungle?

Do you own a chess set?

Names something you thought would be easy but was hard for you.

What was the name of your first pet?

Do you have different groups of friends who seldom or never meet one another?

Can someone be both sane and insane at the same time?

Is everyone equal at birth?

Name three uses for chewing gum.

What do you think about people who hunt animals for entertainment?

What recent news event has captured your interest?

Are NASCAR drivers athletes?

What do you call this: / and this: \ and this: ~?

What is in your favorite sandwich?

How do you decide if your work is good enough?

Would you rather be rich and ugly or poor and good looking?

How many years should a couple date before marrying?

What are your thoughts about Cuba?

Do you swear in front of your parents?

Have you ever been mentioned in a newspaper?

Are you adventurous about trying new foods?

What are your thoughts about the commercialization of sports?

If you could cross a turtle with another animal, what would the other animal be...?

Do you ever Google yourself?

Would you want to be frozen after death with the possibility of being brought back to life in the future?

Should gun owners be required to have insurance?

Can you arch one eyebrow?

What is something that you know and believe without any doubt but cannot prove?

Do you know how to change a tire?

Do you believe in ghosts?

Are you telling the truth if you lie in bed?

How do you think the income tax system could be improved?

What is the best thing about the winter?

If you could remove one word from the English language, what would it be?

Do you usually feel self-confident?

Name a song that often gets stuck in your head.

Is what you know or what you believe more important?

Have you ever seen someone you knew and purposely avoided them?

Do you at times enjoy playing the Devil's advocate?

Do you think wearing motorcycle helmets should be mandatory?

Do you like the smell of fresh coffee?

Would you rather never be alone for a year or always be alone for a year?

Are you nostalgic for anything?

Do you think competition is a good or a bad thing?

Have you ever ridden a mechanical bull?

Do you consider yourself an adventurous person?

Do good things come to those who wait?

What do you think is the most difficult sport to play?

Do your parents have a favorite child?

Would you rather be the clown or ride the bull?

What is the hardest choice you have ever had to make?

What is the longest you have ever stood in line?

Will robots replace humans?

What should the government do to save endangered species?

Would you rather have an extra hour every day or have $10 given to you every day?

What things do you carry with you every day when you leave your home?

Have you ever stolen anything?

Do you have too few or too many choices?

Where were you when you found out about the 9/11 attacks?

When was the last time you got caught in a lie?

Do you judge others by the cars they drive?

If a good friend asked you for the answer to a question during an exam, what would you do?

What is the biggest risk you have ever taken?

Do you like drinking plain water?

What is your favorite flavor of Jell-O?

Have you ever been hypnotized?

Do you like the smell of freshly cut grass?

Have you ever swallowed something strange?

What are your thoughts about athletes doping?

Have you ever taught a pet to do a trick?

Why do you think people are so interested in celebrities?

Is war necessary?

What celebrity irritates you the most?

What problems does the Internet create?

How long do you think you would survive if you had to grow or forage for food?

What is an unusual belief that you hold?

Do you think you would like to be a bartender?

What do you think is the most significant sporting event that has happened in your lifetime?

Have you ever known anyone who wore an ascot (not as a joke)?

Would you teach your child to "hit back" at school if somebody hit him?

New York Yankees or Baltimore Orioles?

How important is it to be able to speak a language in addition to English?

Do you think life is fair?

If you could, what small business would you like to start?

What is your favorite vegetable?

If you were a frog would you rather live as a pet or in the wild?

Do you think that rich people are happier?

What are your thoughts about Groucho Marx?

Have you ever had pet fish?

Do you think you would be a good telemarketer?

Is there something you hate about your home town?

Is there a TV program that you are embarrassed to admit you enjoy?

Given all the health warnings, why do you think people continue to take up smoking?

Should penalties be set or should judges have the right to determine sentences on a case by case basis?

Do you believe in reincarnation?

What is something you disagree with about the way you were raised?

Do children or adults have more freedom?

What is the most overrated book you ever read?

What is something you are glad you tried but will never try again?

Have you ever tried chewing tobacco?

Hamburgers or hotdogs?

If you found out the company you worked for was doing something illegal would you blow the whistle?

If you were the eighth Dwarf, what would your name be?

What would be the title of your autobiography?

What TV game show would you want to go on?

What do you do as soon as you walk in the house after being out?

What is the worst experience you ever had at a restaurant?

What stresses you out?

What are you putting off?

Lima beans, spinach, or peas?

Do you find it hard to say no to people?

What is the most you have ever spent to fill your gas tank?

When you are in a new location do you tend to visit known franchise-type restaurants or mom and pop's?

What is your biggest weakness?

If you could be CEO of any existing company which one would you choose?

What toppings do you like on hotdogs?

Did you attend a high school prom?

Do you think creativity comes with time and effort or are we born with creative talent?

Do you like to garden?

Have you ever spent a night sleeping in a bathtub?

Do you finish what you start?

Who is your role model?

If you were going to purchase a franchise business which one would it be?

Have you ever told a stewardess you have a peanut allergy just to annoy the other passengers?

In what ways has science had a negative impact on society?

Dinner or supper?

Do you feel older or younger than you are?

To what degree are you willing to give up stability to have an interesting life?

What do you think about the expression "It is what it is?"

Who is your idea of a perfect man or woman?

Have you ever had a prayer come true?

What do you think is the most dangerous sport?

What is your least favorite fast food restaurant?

What is the last movie you saw?

Do you hold grudges?

Are you allergic to anything?

Do you think a world with no countries and only one government would be better or worse?

Does the American Dream still exist?

Should cigarette companies be allowed to advertise freely?

If you were a hammer, what would you do?

What is the best thing that has happened to you in the past week?

What are you most skeptical about?

Which Biblical character do you identify with most?

If you had children what would you say to them about using marijuana?

When reading or studying do you like to listen to music or do you prefer silence?

Strawberry or raspberry?

What is the best place in town to go out for breakfast?

Which fictional TV family is most like your own?

Is there someone not related to you that you call Aunt or Uncle?

Convertible sports car or pick-up truck?

How important do you think coaches are in athletics?

Have you ever read anything by Ayn Rand?

If you had a servant come to your home for 1 hour each day, what would you have him or her do?

Do you believe that senior citizens should receive deferential treatment?

Have you ever had a bad case of buyer's remorse after making a purchase?

At what age does a person become old?

Is there something you love about your home town?

If you were offered a chance to only work from your house via computer, would you do it?

If you call in a "to go" order then decide you do not want it are you obligated to pick it up and pay for it?

In what way are thoughts different from feelings?

What is your favorite sandwich?

What do you want to be remembered for?

Have you ever taken advice from a stranger?

If you had the option to know the day and time of your death, would you want to know?

Is torture ever justified?

Do you tend to question conventional wisdom?

What common foods do you refuse to eat?

Does it bother you when different foods touch on your plate?

Would you like to have a pig as a pet?

What is your favorite comic strip?

To what extent should immigrants retain their culture?

Happy Holidays, Merry Christmas, or Seasons Greetings?

What are your thoughts about donating organs for transplant in exchange for money?

Ketchup or mustard?

Would you rather live in LA or NYC?

Have you ever had a panic attack?

What are you an expert at or about?

If you had a band what would you name it?

What is the first thing you do when you wake up?

If you were going to write a fictional book, what would it be about?

Can two people disagree and both be right?

Can you wink with both of your eyes?

If you were called for jury duty would you hope to get selected or to not get selected?

What is something you can do better than anyone else you know?

What is the most valuable thing you have ever won?

If your town was getting a pro football team and you could name it, what would you call it?

Do you have a passport?

Do your parents follow mostly traditional male and female roles?

Would you rather earn a million dollars or win a million dollars?

What do you think is the biggest news event that has happened in your lifetime?

What is the best thing about religion?

Do you typically drive over the speed limit?

Are men better drivers than women?

Do you have a lot of self-discipline?

How do you feel about politicians openly sharing their religious beliefs?

Why do you think people create computer viruses?

How do you feel about your career?

What is the biggest hail you have ever seen?

What is the most delicious food you have ever eaten in your life?

Do you like homemade chocolate chip cookies?

What are your thoughts about the saying "Bless his/her heart?"

Pizza or spaghetti?

Have you ever made a snowman?

What is your favorite frozen dinner?

Do you ever think about packing your bags and leaving everything behind?

Have you ever forgotten something really important?

What would be the advantage or disadvantage of all people speaking the same language?

What are three things each of which you can do in a single second?

Do you like curry?

What do you think when you see people throwing trash on the ground?

What is your favorite city on the US?

Do you like Mexican food?

What is a lesson you learned from a sibling?

Peppermint or spearmint?

What is the most expensive thing you have ever broken?

What is the secret to a happy life?

Should the male always pay for a date?

Do you talk out loud to yourself?

Should marijuana be legalized?

Have you ever witnessed a national news event?

What is the difference between a friend and an acquaintance?

What is your favorite comedy movie?

Who is your favorite Alan?

If you had a racehorse what would you name it?

What uncommon ability do you have?

Do you still consider your parent's house to be home?

What is your favorite Biblical story?

What do you think people in foreign countries learn about the US from movies and TV?

What is the most insensitive thing a person can do?

Would you rather vote for an honest but unwise politician or a dishonest one with a lot of political savvy?

Do you believe most people are honest?

If the job "President of the World" were real, who would you vote for to do it?

If you could add a face to Mt. Rushmore, who would you add?

Do the ends usually justify the means?

Do you prefer having a piece of cake or a cupcake?

Do you think smoking cigarettes should be totally banned?

When did you last climb a tree?

Would you ever consider living abroad?

Do you like lemon meringue pie?

Is there something you promised to have done by now but have not done yet?

Can you juggle?

What is the most interesting gift you have ever received?

If you were a goldfish, what would you want in your tank?

How much do you tip at restaurants?

Do you prefer horns, percussion, or strings?

Should women and children be put in lifeboats first?

At what age should a citizen be allowed to vote?

What is your happiest memory from your childhood?

Can you think of an otherwise banal interaction that you had with a stranger that has impacted you?

What amount of money per month would it take for you to give up your mobile phone forever?

Have you ever had a dog?

What are you seeking in your life?

Do you know the 12 Days of Christmas by heart?

If you had sufficient access to public transportation would you stop driving?

How do you like to spend Sunday mornings?

If you were given free tickets would you attend an opera?

Do children have a responsibility to care for their elderly parents?

Can you think of a time when you did the right thing by listening to your heart and not your head?

The Israelis or the Palestinians?

If you had to be a teacher of something, what would you teach?

What do you think motivates people to commit vandalism?

Should underage children be allowed to drink alcohol in the home?

Are you ever afraid of getting what you want?

What is the most interesting class you ever took?

Are you typically decisive or indecisive?

Can you buy happiness (to any extent)?

Do you push elevator buttons more than once when they seem slow?

Are you more afraid of snakes or spiders?

Who in your family would make the best president?

In what way do you hope you are like your mother?

Would you rather be a bus driver or a ranch hand?

Would you rather be strong, rich, or smart?

If you were on a team, what number would you want on your jersey?

What historical period would you like to live in if you could go back in time?

How do you behave when you are angry?

Where would you want to retire to?

_____

What is the most wasteful thing that you normally do?

_____

Elevator or stairs?

_____

What are your thoughts about Ernest Hemmingway?

_____

If you could have asked Jesus one question, what would it have been?

_____

Do you think it is okay for vegetables to be genetically modified?

_____

How well do you know yourself?

_____

Are you comfortable eating in a restaurant or going to the movies alone?

_____

What was your least favorite subject in school?

_____

What is the worst thing about religion?

If you could be invisible for a day, what would you do?

Would you like to live forever?

Was Jesus a capitalist?

Should tax money be used to fund the arts?

What do you like on baked potatoes?

What is one thing you have tried to change about yourself, but couldn't?

Can you think of 3 countries that do not have the letter "a" in their names?

What do you do when a vending machine keeps your money without dispensing your purchase?

Who did you idolize growing up?

Is 1 plus 1 always 2?

Under what circumstances are you most likely to procrastinate?

Should video cameras be in every courtroom?

Would you rather own a sailboat or a speedboat?

Is walking on hot coals something everyone can do or is it some sort of trick?

What was the hardest test you have ever taken?

Have you lied to your parents recently?

Have you ever played golf?

What is your favorite breed of dog?

Would you rather live life as a bird or a fish?

Assuming all living creatures were safe, what would you take if your home was on fire?

Are there any movies you can watch over and over?

What would a chameleon look like if surrounded by mirrors?

Can equality exist in a free society?

Do you like fireplaces?

Have you ever (seriously) wanted to write a book?

Aisle or window seat?

Should felons be allowed to vote?

What is the most important thing taught to you by your parents?

Do you like pulp in your OJ?

Without looking it up do you know who Ferdinand Lewis Alcindor, Jr. is?

When you are at the grocery store do you use the self checkout?

Would you rather always lose or never play?

Why do you think there are so many ads on TV for automobile insurance?

What is your main goal in life?

Do you know how to surf?

Should people receiving public assistance be required to undergo drug testing?

What acronym is used most frequently at your job?

When was the last time you ate ramen noodles?

At heart are you a spender or a saver?

What does it mean to be an adult?

Do you ever buy uncomfortable clothes just because they look good?

What one word best describes the USA?

Green beans or lima beans?

Do you think it would be good to do away with national currencies and have one world-wide currency instead?

Would you rather be a bee or a lizard?

What is the biggest factor that influences the decisions you make?

Would you rather be an accountant or an electrician?

Is there a sport you love to play but hate to watch?

What is intimacy for you?

What is normally the highlight of your day?

Do you find it hard to admit when you are wrong?

What is something nobody could steal from you?

If you were building an ark but could only fit 5 sets of animals on it, which ones would you choose?

Would you rather be a mailman or a UPS driver?

What do you wish you had done over the weekend that you did not do?

Would you say your life is simple or complicated?

Have you ever acted on stage?

What would you do if you learned that your child was being bullied in school?

If you could be "reincarnated" as any non-living thing, what would you want to be?

If you were going to put a message in a bottle and toss it in the ocean what would that message say?

Can you name all the US vice presidents since 1961?

Would you prefer to be a prosecutor or a defense attorney?

Do you believe in evolution?

Would you rather be an author or an editor?

What does it mean to be a man?

If you were sand, what would you say to people on the beach?

Have you ever been rushed by an ambulance into the emergency room?

What is your most vivid memory of elementary school?

As a child what was your favorite piece of playground equipment?

Do you like black licorice?

Have you ever been stung by a bee?

What is your favorite breakfast food?

What are three things a brick can be used for?

What is the worst part of your job?

If you were invited to a potluck what would you bring?

What makes a good driver?

Do you like yogurt?

What sports would you rather watch on TV than see in person?

What are your thoughts about vegetarianism?

Are you a different person now than you were 5 years ago?

What is the hottest you have ever been?

Do you ever have energy drinks?

Who do you admire the most?

What is something that you know but wish you didn't know?

What is the best way to relax?

What is your favorite way to waste time at work without getting caught?

Pedigreed or mutt?

What is your philosophy in life?

What are your views about the use of animals in medical experiments?

Would you eat any of the following: dogs, insects, monkeys, raccoons, spiders, or snake?

What personality trait gets you into the most trouble?

Would you like to be famous?

If your name was William, would you go by William, Will, Willie, Bill, or Billy?

Is there a word or words that you typically mispronounce?

Do you have any childhood friendships that are still strong today?

Can you touch your tongue to your nose?

Have you ever fallen asleep or almost fallen asleep while driving?

What three living people would you most like to meet?

Have you ever pretended something was still new so you could return it even though you had used it?

If your name was Robert, would you go by Robert, Rob, Bobby, or Robby?

Are the best things in life free?

Have you ever been treated by a chiropractor?

Frank Sinatra, Elvis Presley, or The Beatles?

Would you rather live to be 90 but have a boring life or live to be 35 and have lots of excitement?

Are you good at fixing things around the house?

Have you ever had an incident because you overslept?

What is the most money you have ever wasted on something silly?

Do you prefer to play team sports or to work out on your own?

Why do you think people get so excited about pro sports?

Would you rather have a broken toe or a broken finger?

Is free will different from freedom?

What would you do with your time if you only had one year left to live?

Did you, or do you, know any of your grandparents?

Has anything ever taken your breath away?

Have you ever gone to a professional baseball game?

Name three items that can always be found in your refrigerator.

Would you rather be named Abraham or George?

If you got a new job what would you miss most about the one you have now?

What is your favorite commercial?

Can you name all 50 states?

Do you ever read your horoscope?

When you walk into a room what is the first thing you typically notice?

Have you ever milked a cow?

Should stores be open on holidays?

Can you drive a manual shift car?

If you were on a plane and the pilots died, do you think you could land it if given instructions by radio?

If you were a secret agent what would you want your code name to be?

Would you rather drive an ice-cream truck and listen to Pop Goes the Weasel over and over or be on welfare?

Is there such a thing as being too honest?

Would you turn in one of your siblings if you knew he/she had committed a crime?

What do you think should be done to keep people who are under the influence of alcohol off the road?

Is there a part of your life that seems to have taken over?

What do you think are the three greatest inventions of all time?

How do you tell if someone is lying to you?

What rule did you most disagree with growing up?

Should global concerns be valued over national concerns?

What do you think about gun control?

Do you prefer soap powders/ detergents/ deodorants to be scented or unscented?

At what age does adulthood start?

If you had space for a small garden what would you plant?

What is the difference between a terrorist and a freedom fighter?

What do you order at Italian restaurants?

If there was a televised execution would you watch it?

Can you ride a motorcycle?

Would you rather be a policeman or fireman?

What are your thoughts about Bob Dylan?

If you got into a cab and found a file on the floor marked Top Secret, what would you do?

Do you think it is a good idea to try to bring back extinct species like dinosaurs?

What is your favorite season?

What is the worst experience you have ever had while eating out?

What would you do if you saw a friend littering?

Do you prefer wallpaper or paint?

Should the government fund public radio and TV?

Have you ever sleepwalked?

What is something you can do that looks easier than it is.

What do you think would be the worst part about being in prison?

What is your favorite vegetable?

Do you typically make a list before going shopping?

Do you think elderly drivers should undergo extra testing to be permitted to continue driving?

Do you find it difficult to change?

If you were to create a sport, what would it entail?

When was the last time you got stopped by a cop or pulled over?

What do you typically order at Chinese restaurants?

What are your thoughts about recycling?

If you were a zebra would you rather live at a zoo or in the wild?

What is your favorite fast food restaurant?

Are you left or right handed?

Do you think letting parents to choose the gender and traits of their babies is interfering with evolution?

Do you think cell phones cause cancer?

What is your least favorite vegetable?

What is your opinion of state-sponsored gambling?

What is the strangest place you have ever fallen asleep?

What is your favorite guitar riff?

How do you relieve stress?

What is your favorite topic of discussion?

Is conflict inevitable?

Which member of your family has had the greatest influence on your current way of thinking?

Do you hate anyone?

What is something your mother used to often make for dinner that you dislike?

If you could put any message and picture on a billboard what would you put?

If you were in charge of speed limits what would you choose for highways?

Can you do any martial arts?

Have you ever picked apples?

Have you ever failed an important quiz or test?

Do you think famous people should accept being approached by their fans at all times?

What is the worst movie you have seen recently in a theater?

Would you rather be able to see into your future or to change your past?

How would you describe your family to someone you just met using less than ten words?

If you had an accident and your body was destroyed, would you let doctors put your brain in a robot?

How do you typically spend Christmas Eve?

Do you like to be O or X in Tic Tac Toe?

What age do you hope to live to?

How would you prevent people from dropping out of high school?

Do you think spending tax dollars on space exploration is a wise use of money?

If you could coach any sport, which would you choose?

What is your favorite spice?

Would you rather be able to fly or become invisible?

What is the easiest money you have ever earned?

Do you think overweight people are discriminated against?

If you were torturing someone with music, what is the one track you would play on repeat for days on end?

In a blind taste test do you think you could identify Coke, Pepsi, and RC sodas?

Which would you rather: earn a PhD, win an Olympic Medal, or write a best seller?

Have you ever been very lost?

How important is it to you that others are on time?

Would you rather be a police officer or an actor?

What do you think of boxing?

What was the most mischievous thing you did as a child?

What do you think is included in the definitive American meal?

If someone looked in your top dresser drawer, what would they learn about you?

Should speaking on a cell phone while driving be illegal?

Would you rather live life without emotional pain or without physical pain?

What would you do if 500 mice just escaped from their cages in a pet shop where you worked?

Should telemarketing be banned?

Do you have good memory for numbers?

How could gang violence be ended?

Have you ever jet skied?

Do you like bacon?

If you could eliminate one odor from earth what would it be?

If you were a professional wrestler what would your stage name be?

New York Yankees or Boston Red Sox?

Are there things that you got away with as a teen that your parents still do not know about?

What do you think about animals in circuses?

Which is more important, mercy or justice?

Have you ever had to let go of a dream?

Are you optimistic about the future?

What is the most frightening encounter you have had with a wild animal?

Is there a formula for happiness?

Would you rather be rich and obese or poor and in terrific shape?

How does who you are compare with who you want to be?

When was the last time you bought new jeans?

Does your family have any Christmas traditions?

Can you whistle?

What hobbies did you have a child?

When was the first time you saw the ocean?

Have you ever really not been able to find your car in a big parking lot or garage?

What is something children are not usually allowed to do, which you think they should be allowed to do?

Who taught you to drive?

Have you ever been bitten by a dog?

What did you want to be when you grew up?

Have you ever gone to a professional basketball game?

Should a single man or woman be able to adopt a child?

Have you ever had a black eye?

Are you concerned about global warming?

Have you ever hitchhiked?

Should all homes be connected to the Internet?

How do you like your hotdogs cooked (grilled, boiled...)?

What are you most grateful for?

Did your mom or dad ever make you wear something you hated?

Are there any reality television shows you enjoy watching?

Would you rather be addicted to alcohol or to gambling?

Can you eat (properly) with chopsticks?

Do you like April Fool's Day?

Would you be willing to die for your country?

Would you like to visit Alaska?

If you had a parrot, what is the first thing you would try to teach him/her to say?

Do you own any band t-shirts?

If a movie was being made of your life and you could choose the actor to play you, who would you choose?

What are your thoughts about Pink Floyd?

Do you ever drink milk or juice straight from containers while standing at the refrigerator door?

What are your thoughts about Jack Nicholson?

Do you like the smell of new cars?

Would you rather have to sit all day or stand all day?

What is the craziest thing you believed as a child?

Would you ever run for political office?

Would you rather drive a beat-up car that runs well, or a beautiful car that breaks down a lot?

Can you read music?

Have you ever been the victim of a crime?

Who is the funniest person you know?

Is art created using a computer less artistic or meaningful than art created by hand?

Do you know any rap song lyrics by heart?

What are your thoughts about how schools should handle bullying?

How frequently do you use Wikipedia?

Should there be a cap on how much athletes can earn?

Do you often sing along when you are alone and listening to music?

What do you think about househusbands?

What is the weirdest food you have ever been offered and did you eat it?

Do you own any clothes that are completely warn out but you refuse to throw out?

What is your earliest memory?

What is your favorite brand of breakfast cereal?

What do you think of when you think of a hero?

Have you ever broken someone's heart?

Do you ever buy second-hand things?

If you could have dinner with John Kennedy, John Lennon, or John Adams who would you choose?

What is the dumbest commercial you have seen lately?

If a waiter undercharges you do you give a bigger tip?

If you could meet someone famous, who would it be?

If you had a frog and could train it to do one trick, what would you train it to do?

If you could trade lives with somebody you know, who would it be?

If you could witness any past event, what would it be?

What was the make of your first car?

Do you have a good luck charm?

Did you ever set fire to something and had to call the fire department?

Do you know how to play poker?

Who is the most successful person you know?

Have you ever won a trophy?

If you found nude pictures of a friend on the Internet would you tell him/her?

Have you ever eaten frogs' legs?

How long do you think you would tolerate solitary confinement?

Did you ever watch Mr. Roger's Neighborhood?

What do you think makes a great coach?

Do you frequently lose or misplace things?

Why do you think so many popular singers die when young?

Do you talk on your cell phone when socializing or dining with people in person?

What Guinness World Record do you think you could win?

Baked, mashed, or fried potatoes?

Are zebras black with white stripes, or white with black stripes?

Do you have all your wisdom teeth?

Are you a good cook?

Would you prefer a society with art but not science or science but not art?

What is one thing that you do not understand about your parents?

If you were planning to buy a pair of jeans what store would you go to?

Do you have a collection of anything?

What makes you feel young?

What breakfast food do you like to eat for dinner?

What freedoms do you value most?

Overall, do you live for tomorrow or today?

Are there certain things journalists should not report on?

Should cigarette companies be legally liable for smokers who die from lung cancer?

If you were posing for a caricature of yourself, what feature do you think the artist would stress?

Do you sleep with the TV on?

What is the worst injury you have ever had?

How did you learn to swim?

What things in life should always be free?

Have you ever gone sailing?

Can you think of something you really wanted but then never used once you had it?

What would you do if you got a marble stuck in your nostril?

Should undocumented immigrants be given free health care?

Can you think of a time when you arrived at a place or event and were completely under or over-dressed?

Have you ever seen something which you could just not explain?

What is changing in your life right now?

If you were to become a vegetarian what one food would you miss the most?

What are things that you wish people knew about you without your having to tell them?

Should drug users be given tax-payer purchased needles?

What role does exercise play in your life?

What is the difference between crime and sin?

Why do people take illegal drugs?

What would you do if you saw a sleeping stranger on a beach getting a serious sunburn?

Do you eat the cake or the frosting first?

When alone do you set a table and eat or do you just sit in front of the TV or a computer?

Would you rather die or get imprisoned for 100 years?

Do you own any pro-team jerseys?

Do you think divorces should be easy or difficult to get?

Have you ever been in a restaurant that offered a prize for eating all of something and tried to do it?

Would you rather be the worst player on the best team or the best player on a lousy team?

What are your thoughts about a flat tax?

Do you think more about the future or the past?

Would you break a law that you consider to be unjust?

Would you rather be a dentist or a podiatrist?

What is the biggest thing you have ever changed your mind about?

What is under your bed?

Do you typically prefer hot, room temperature, cold, iced, or frozen beverages?

Would you have any misgivings about going into business with one of your siblings?

Chicago Bulls or Miami Heat?

Who do you think really controls the US?

Cat or dog?

Do you finish your taxes as soon as possible or wait for April 14th?

Where do you like to sit in movie cinemas?

How many licks to get to the center or a Tootsie Pop?

Which breed of dog do you think is the smartest?

Do you usually eat everything on your plate?

What is your all-time favorite movie?

Is there a difference between one's mind and one's brain?

Would you rather climb a mountain or read a great book?

How should people react to racial epithets?

What is something that you have never done but think you would be good at?

Do you tend to take on the problems of those around you?

What chore do you enjoy that most people hate?

If you had a warning label, what would yours say?

Do you own an e-reader of any sort?

Would you like to visit Africa?

What are your thoughts about Andy Warhol?

Have you ever fallen down a flight of stairs?

If you were stuck 20 feet in the air at the end of a day alone on a ski lift, what would you do?

What is your definition of wealthy?

Chicago Bears or Green Bay Packers?

What would you like to be remembered for?

Do you like Earl Grey Tea?

What are your thoughts about metal detectors in schools?

What is something that you never did as a kid because you were worried about what others would think?

What is your favorite candy?

Even or odd?

Can you name all 7 dwarfs?

What is another word for synonym?

What do you think about cloning?

Do you like Rice Crispy Treats?

Who is the greatest living American athlete?

If your life had a soundtrack, what would it be?

Can you tolerate eating very hot peppers?

What do you do most when you are bored?

What is your favorite zoo animal?

Did you ever go to camp?

Are you happy with where you are in life?

Have you ever said "I love you" and not meant it?

Are you good at keeping secrets?

What do you think of airport security?

ABOUT THE AUTHOR

Dr. Valerie Christie is dangerously over-educated. She holds a Doctor of Education degree in Higher Education from Florida State University, a Master of Education in Learning Systems Design & Development from University of Missouri at Columbia, a Master of Education in Educational Studies from River College, a Master of Science in Business Education from New Hampshire College of Southern New Hampshire University, a Master of Management in Engineering Management from the University of Dallas, an MBA in Marketing from the University of Dallas, a Master of Library Science from Texas Woman's University, a Master of International Studies in Security Studies from Troy State University, a Master of Science in Human Behavior and Business from Amberton University, a Master of Science in Psychology from Capella University, a Bachelor of Arts in American Studies from Rivier College, and a Certificate in Paralegal Studies from the University of North Texas.

Dr. Christie lives in Texas where she is a student and continues asking more and more questions. Her interests include 1960's kitsch, animal rights, The Beatles, Fred Basset comic strips, and factory tours.

11/19
3

CPSIA information can be obtained at www.ICGtesting.com
Printed in the USA
LVOW13s2129050314

376241LV00001B/146/P